IN THEORY
IT'S EASY!

IN THEORY IT'S EASY!

Naomi Phillips

authorHOUSE®

AuthorHouse™
1663 Liberty Drive
Bloomington, IN 47403
www.authorhouse.com
Phone: 1-800-839-8640

Published by AuthorHouse   08/13/2012

ISBN: 978-1-4772-2578-3 (sc)
ISBN: 978-1-4772-2580-6 (e)

CONTENTS

Chapter 1 - Where to Begin 1

Chapter 2 - All about notes 7

Chapter 3 - Time and major scales 19

Chapter 4 - Minor Scales 35

Chapter 5 - Building diatonic chords 51

Music Terminology Index 58

Bibliography 60

A Big Thank you to my parents for all the support they have always shown me, to my partner Lee for the moral support and for Tregs for always believing in me even when I didn't believe in myself!

CHAPTER ONE

Where to Begin

Where to Begin?

Music theory can be like a minefield to the novice with many people not knowing where to begin. Theory is like learning to read a new language, the language of music, so where better to begin than at the beginning?

Music is written on what is called a staff; on this it tells us what <u>key</u> we are playing in, what notes to play and for how long.

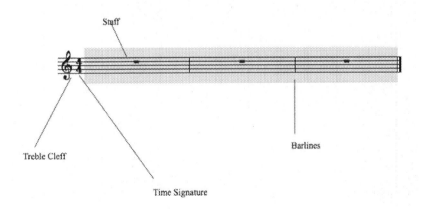

The lines on which we write our notes are called a staff. The clefs (see above) tell us the notes names for on and in between the lines. Lets see what the names of the notes become for the treble clef.

E   F   G   A   B   C   D   E

The notes for the bass clef are as follows:—

Bass   G   A   B   C   D   E   F   G

There is one particular note that does not go on the staff but instead sits outside. This note is called MIDDLE C. It is called this, as it is the note closest to the middle of the piano. It is written as follows:—

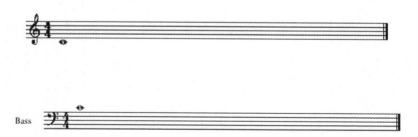

Practice Questions 1

1) Name the following on the staff:—

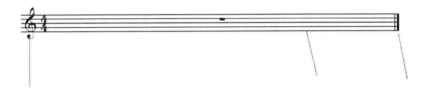

2) Name the notes below:—

3) Put the correct clef (bass or treble) to match each note.

CHAPTER TWO

All about notes

The following are two diagrams, one of a bass guitar and what frets correspond to which note, and one of a piano, showing which keys correspond to which notes.

BASS GUITAR DIAGRAM

OPEN	E	A	D	G
	F	A#/Bb	D#/Eb	G#/Ab
	F#/Gb	B	E	A
•3rd fret	G	C	F	A#/Bb
	G#/Ab	C#/Db	F#/Gb	B
•5th fret	A	D	G	C
	A#/Bb	D#/Eb	G#/Ab	C#/Db
•7th fret	B	E	A	D
	C	F	A#/Bb	D#/Eb
•9th fret	C#/Db	F#/Gb	B	E
	D	G	C	F
	D#/Eb	G#/Ab	C#/Db	F#/Gb
•12th fret	E	A	D	G

When reading notation the following example shows you what fret numbers relate to the notes on the bass clef, using the respective strings E, A, D and G.

PIANO DIAGRAM

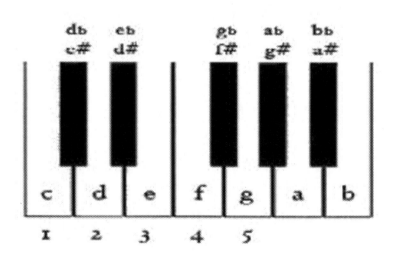

Naomi Phillips

Tones and Semitones

Tone - or note, a sound of definite pitch.

Semitone - normally the smallest notated pitch difference in music—for instance G-G sharp.

A tone can be seen as two steps if we refer to our diagrams of the notes on the piano/bass guitar.

It takes two steps from C-D (C# in the middle) therefore there is a **tone** difference. However there is only one step from C-C# making this a **semitone** in difference.

So far we have looked at what are called natural notes but now we can see there are other notes, sharps and flats. We will now see how they are written on the staff.

<u>Sharps, flats and naturals</u>

For a musician to know whether the note is to be played as a sharp or a flat we use these two symbols:—
\# = Sharp
b = flat

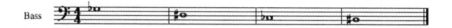

As you can see from the above example the symbol is always placed before the note to be played so you know what note to play before you get to it.

When sharps and flats are placed in a piece of music they are known as "accidentals".

When a sharp or flat is placed in front of a note in a piece of music, it means that every note of the same in that bar is to be played that way until the natural symbol is shown. Then you revert back to playing the notes as natural notes. Below is an example of how this is written.

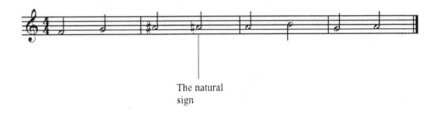

The natural
sign

The Value of Notes

The length (or duration) of each note is indicated by different shaped notes. Signs called rests indicate silent periods during a piece of music.

Note	Shape	Rest	Value in Terms of a Semibreve	Corresponding Names used in America
Semibreve			1	Whole note
Minim			1/2	Half note
Crotchet			1/4	Quarter note
Quaver			1/8	Eight note
Semi Quaver			1/16	Sixteenth note
Demi Semi Quaver			1/32	Thirty second note

Naomi Phillips

The next table shows how many numbers of different notes are contained in one semibreve:—

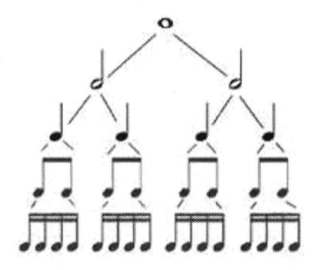

Practice Questions 2

1) Write if there is a tone or semitone difference between the notes below:— (if you need to, refer back to your piano or guitar diagrams)

2) With the following notes, draw in the corresponding symbol:—

3) Draw the following notes and their corresponding rests:—
   a)   Semibreve
   b)   Minim:—
   c)   Crotchet:—
   d)   Semiquaver:—
   e)   Demisemiquaver:—

4) How many crotchets are in a minim?
5) How many semiquavers are in a crotchet?
6) How many minims are in a semibreve?
7) How many semiquavers are in a quaver?

CHAPTER THREE

Time and major scales

Dotted notes and ties

A dot can be added onto the end of a note or rest in order to increase its length by half again. For example a dotted crotchet would be played for the length of a crotchet plus a quaver, or is equal in length to three quavers.
A tie can also be used to increase the length of a note. Only the first note is sounded but is held for the duration of both notes.

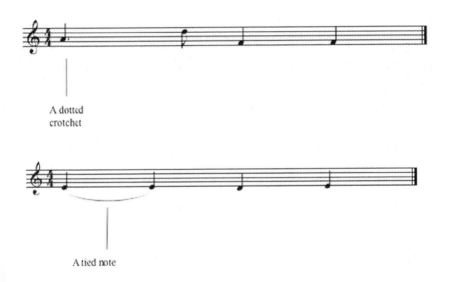

A dotted crotchet

A tied note

Basic Time Signatures

Definition:—A sign is usually consisting of two figures, one above the other, the upper figure representing the number of beats per bar and the lower one the time value of each beat. This sign is placed after the key signature at the outset of a piece or a section of music.
http://dictionary.reference.com/browse/time+signature (9/5/2011)

So if the time signature is 2/4 it means there are two beats in each bar equaling to crotchet beats.

The following table shows **Simple Time Signatures.**

Simple duple 2 beats in a bar	**Simple triple** 3 beats in a bar	**Simple quadruple** 4 beats in a bar
2/2 ♩ ♩	3/2 ♩ ♩ ♩	4/2 4 minim beats
2/4 ♩ ♩	3/4 ♩ ♩ ♩	4/4 4 crotchet beats
2/8 ♪ ♪	3/8 ♪ ♪ ♪	4/8 4 quaver beats

Major Scales

Definition:— "A diatonic scale having half steps (semitones) between the third and fourth and the seventh and eighth degrees and whole steps (tones) between the other adjacent degree."
http://www.thefreedictionary.com/major+scale (11/5/2011)

In the C major scale we can see the semitone difference in the third and fourth degree being between the notes E and F, and we can see the difference in the seventh and eighth degrees between the notes B and C. On the following page will be a list of all the major scales. It is really just a case of playing, learning and familiarizing yourself with each one.

All The Major Scales

G Major
G A B C D E F# G
D Major
D E F# G A B C# D
A Major
A B C# D E F# G# A
E Major
E F# G# A B C D# E
B Major
B C# D# E F# G# A# B
F# Major
F# G# A# B C# D# E# F#
C# Major
C# D# E# F# G# A# B# C#

F Major
F G A Bb C D E F
Bb Major
Bb C D Eb F G A Bb

Eb Major

Eb F G Ab Bb C D Eb

Ab Major

Ab Bb C Db Eb F G Ab

Db Major

Db Eb F Gb Ab Bb C Db

Gb Major

Gb Ab Bb Cb Db Eb F Gb

Cb Major

Cb Db Eb Fb Gb Ab Bb Cb

The Scale of C Major has no sharps and no flats.

<u>Key Signatures</u>

So a player knows what scale or key they are playing in, a key signature is used at the beginning of a piece of music. This also helps to make the music easier to read, as there are not numerous accidentals throughout the whole piece making it difficult to read. Below are the key signatures for all the major scales.

G Major

D Major

A Major

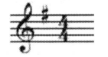

E Major

B Major

F# Major

C# Major

Key signatures continued . . .

F Major

Bb Major

Eb Major

Ab Major

Db Major

Gb Major

Cb Major

Key Signatures in Bass Clef

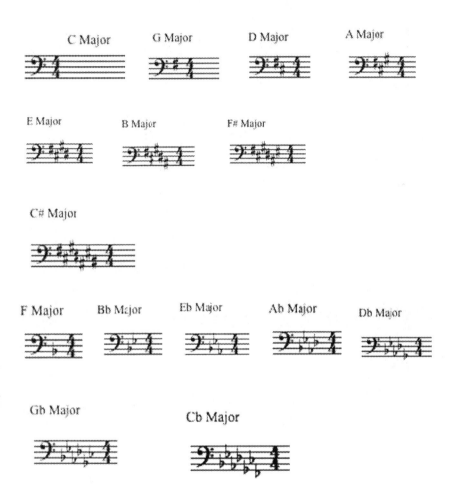

When playing in any scale the key signature is to be followed. For example in the scale of G major (which has one sharp F#) every F which is read must be played as F# unless an accidental is in place.

Now that we have looked at time signatures and key signatures let us have a look at these within a piece of music.

Let us break down the above piece of music to make sense of it:—

1) Firstly we can see we are reading the notes from the treble clef
2) Looking at the key signature we ca see it has two sharps meaning it is D major. The two sharps are F# and C# meaning any note that is a C or an F must be played sharpened.
3) Next we can see the time signature 2/4. As we know, this is two beats in a bar counting in crotchets.
4) It is important that the notes used are grouped into the amounts of beats we are counting in. In the above example we can see the two separate beats in each bar
- Bar 1-2 Crotchets placed separately

- Bar 2-4 Quavers. As two quavers are equal to one crotchet they are placed as two together.
- Bar 3-8 Semiquavers. As four semiquavers are equal to one crotchet they are placed in two groups of four.
- Bar 4-1 Minim. As one minim is equal to two crotchets it is placed on its own in the bar.

Practice Questions 3

1) Fill in the gaps in the following sentences:—
a) The time signature 2/8 has beats, counting in notes.
b) The time signature 3/4 has beats, counting in notes.
c) The time signature 4/2 has beats, counting in notes.

2) How many sharps of flats are in the following scales? Also state whether it is sharps or flats after the amount.
a)   G major
b)   F major
c)   Ab major
d)   B major
e)   C major

3) The sharps F# and C# only belong to which scale?

Naomi Phillips

4) The flats Bb, Eb, Ab, and Db only belong to which scale?

5) In the following examples of key signatures write which scale they are.

CHAPTER FOUR

Minor Scales

Minor Scales

There are three types of minor scales.

1) Natural or Relative minor scale
2) Harmonic minor scales
3) Melodic Minor scale.

Firstly we will look at the natural or melodic minor scale.

Each major scale has a relative minor scale, meaning that the minor scale follows the same key signature as its relative major scale.
To work out each major scales relative minor scale you count to the sixth note of the major scale and that then is its relative minor scale.

Let us have a look at some examples.

C D E F G A B C
1 2 3 4 5 6 7 8

If we take the C major scale and count to its sixth note we get to A. So C majors relative minor scale is A.

So following the key signature of C major with no sharps or flats the notes are as follows:—

A B C D E F G A

If you play this on your instrument you will find it sounds "mournful" or sad.

Let us take a look at another example. Lets use D major as an example this time.

D E F# G A B C# D
1 2 3 4 5 6 7 8

As we can see D majors relative minor scale is B minor. B minor follows the same key signature as D major so the notes for B minor are:—

B C# D E F# G A B

On the following page is a table showing all the major scales alongside their relative minor scales.

Major Scales with their relative Minor Scales	Name and Number of Sharps	Name and Number of Flats
C Major/A Minor	0	0
G Major/E Minor	1 F#	0
D Major/B Minor	2 F#C#	0
A Major/F# Minor	3 F#C#G#	0
E Major/C# Minor	4 F#C#G#D#	0
B Major/G# Minor	5 F#C#G#D#A#	0
F# Major/D# Minor	6 F#C#G#D# A#E#	0
C# Major/A# Minor	7 F#C#G#D# A#E#B#	0
F Major/D Minor	0	1 Bb
Bb Major/G Minor	0	2 BbEb
Eb Major/C Minor	0	3 BbEbAb
Ab Major/F Minor	0	4 BbEbAbDb
Db Major/Bb Minor	0	5 BbEbAbDbGb
Gb Major/Eb Minor	0	6 BbEbAbDb GbCb
Cb Major/Ab Minor	0	7 BbEbAbDbGb CbFb

Practice Question 4(a)

1) Fill in the missing words in the following sentence:—
   Every major scale has a   or minor scale.

2) Which note of the major scale do we count to, to find its relative minor scale?

3) What words could you use to describe the sound when playing a minor scale?

4) Write the relative minor scales of each major scale below:—
   a)   C major
   b)   F major
   c)   D major
   d)   C# major
   e)   Eb major

5) Write out the notes of each of the following minor scales:—
   a)   C minor
   b)   Bb minor
   c)   E minor
   d)   D# minor
   e)   G minor

Harmonic and
Melodic Minor Scales

First lets look at the harmonic minor scale. The Harmonic scale is built by using the same notes as its relative major scale except you raise the seventh note by a semitone. Lets compare a couple of examples so we can see how this works. If you remember A natural minor follows the same key signature as C major so it is written as follows:—

A B C D E F G A

For A harmonic minor we now raise the seventh note of the scale, thus it is written as follows:—

A B C D E F G# A

The next is a more confusing situation. Ab Minor scale:—

Ab Bb Cb Db Eb Fb Gb Ab

When the 7th note is a flat it then turns into a natural, thus Ab harmonic minor is written as follows:—

Ab Bb Cb Db Eb Fb G Ab

The Harmonic minor scale is mainly used for writing harmonies. This is perhaps, because the raised seventh note makes it want to jump to the tonic.

Melodic Minor Scales

The Melodic Minor has two accidentals. On the way up the scale the 6th and 7th notes are sharpened. So A melodic minor would look as follows:—

A B C D E F# G# A

However when playing back down the scale the 6th and 7th notes then return to the same as the natural minor. So written in full A melodic minor would look as follows:—

A B C D E F# G# A G F E D C B A

The melodic minor scale is used mainly for writing melodies. This is because the raised 6th note makes a smoother sounding transition from the 6th to 7th note than in the harmonic minor scale.

Practice Questions (4b)

1) What is the harmonic minor scale usually used for?
2) What is the melodic minor scale usually used for?
3) Which note is altered in the harmonic minor scale?
4) Write out the notes for the following harmonic minor scales:—
   a)   A harmonic minor
   b)   C harmonic minor
   c)   Bb harmonic minor
5) Which notes are altered in the melodic minor scale?
6) How do these notes alter from going up the scale to coming back down the scale?
7) Write out the notes for the following melodic minor scales (going both up and back down the scale):—
   a)   A melodic minor
   b)   E melodic minor
   c)   G melodic minor

Naomi Phillips

Pentatonic Scales

Pentatonic scales are made up of five notes. There are two types of pentatonic scale, the major pentatonic and the natural minor pentatonic. These scales are used in improvising solos, as the notes used are least likely to sound wrong.

Major Pentatonic

To build the major pentatonic scale you use notes 1, 2, 3, 5 and 6 of the major scale. Lets build a couple of major pentatonic scales.

C Major Pentatonic
Firstly we know we are using notes from the scale of C Major so lets write those notes down:—

C D E F G A B C

Secondly we know we are going to use notes 1, 2, 3, 5 and 6, so lets underline those notes

<u>C</u> <u>D</u> <u>E</u> F <u>G</u> <u>A</u> B <u>C</u>
1 2 3 4 5 6 7 1

Now we can write out the scale of C major pentatonic:—

C D E G A C

Lets take a look at one more example before we move on.

A Major Pentatonic
Firstly we know we are using notes from the A major scale so lets write those notes down:—

A B C# D E F# G# A

Secondly we know we are going to use notes 1, 2, 3, 5 and 6, so lets underline those notes.

A̲ B̲ C̲#̲ D E̲ F̲#̲ G# A̲
1 2 3 4 5 6 7 1

Now we can write out the scale of A major pentatonic:—

A B C# E F# A

Minor Pentatonic

To build the minor pentatonic scale you use notes 1, 3, 4, 5 and 7 of the natural minor scale. Lets build a couple of minor pentatonic scales.

A Minor Pentatonic
Firstly we know we are using notes from the scale of A natural minor so lets write these notes down.

A B C D E F G A
Secondly we know we are using notes 1, 3, 4, 5 and 7 so lets underline these notes.

<u>A</u> B <u>C</u> <u>D</u> <u>E</u> F <u>G</u> <u>A</u>
1 2 3 4 5 6 7 8

Now we can write out the notes of the A minor pentatonic scale:—

A C D E G A

Lets have a look at one more example of a minor pentatonic scale.

E Minor Pentatonic

Ok, so we know we are using the notes from the scale of E natural minor. So lets write these down:—

E F# G A B C D E

Secondly we know we are using notes 1, 3, 4, 5 and 7 so lets underline those notes.

<u>E</u> F# <u>G</u> <u>A</u> <u>B</u> C <u>D</u> E
1 2 3 4 5 6 7 8

Now we have the notes of E minor Pentatonic.

E G A B D E

Practice Questions (4c)

1) When do pentatonic scales tend to be used?
2) What are the two types of pentatonic scales?
3) Which notes are used to build a major pentatonic (the numbers of the scale)?
4) Write out the notes for the following pentatonic scales:—
   a)   C major pentatonic
   b)   E major pentatonic
   c)   Ab major pentatonic
5) Which notes are used to build a minor pentatonic (the numbers of the scale)?
   a)   A minor pentatonic
   b)   D minor pentatonic
   c)   B minor pentatonic

CHAPTER FIVE

Building diatonic chords

Building Basic Chords

A chord is made up of three or more notes. This is called a triad.

On our first diagram we can see the bottom notes are the C major scale. Taking the first triad we can see there are three notes placed one on top of each other. The three notes placed in this manner are called a triad.

A triad

Taking the first triad we can see that the notes are C E and G, this makes up the chord of C major.

To build a triad we use a starting note in this case C, miss a note to get E then miss another note to get G. When building our chords we follow the key signature. As we can see from above we are in the Key of C and therefore there are no sharps of flats.

In our next example we can see we have built triads in the scale of G major. Take a look at the third triad, what notes are used? B D and F#. Remember we are in the scale of G major so every F that occurs in the triads or chords will be an F#.

    I   II   III IV   V   VI VII   I

All the chords we have looked at so far are what are known as diatonic chords. This is because they occur naturally by building on the notes of each major scale.

Under each triad we can see that there is a roman numeral. Each of these roman numerals indicates whether the triad (chord) is major in its sounding, or minor in its sounding. Below is a table showing which numeral corresponds to each type of chord.

Naomi Phillips

Roman Numeral	Major or Minor
I	Major
II	Minor
III	Minor
IV	Major
V	Major
VI	Minor
VII	Diminished

The following table will show the sounds corresponding to each Roman numeral in the natural minor scale.

Roman Numeral	Major or Minor
I	Minor
II	Diminished
III	Major
IV	Minor
V	Minor
VI	Major
VII	Minor

Practice Questions 5

1) The three notes that build up a chord are known as what?
2) Write out all the notes of the chords for the C major scale. For example the first chord would be C, E, G.
3) Draw all the triads for the C major scale in both treble and bass clef.
4) Draw all the triads for the Gb major scale in both treble and bass clef.
5) Write out all the notes of the chords for the Gb major scale.
6) The chords we have looked at so far are known as chords.
7) Next to each roman numeral write whether the corresponding chord from a major scale would sound major or minor
   a)   I
   b)   II
   c)   III
   d)   IV

e) V
f) VI
g) VII
8) Next to each roman numeral write whether the corresponding chord from a minor scale would sound major or minor
a) I
b) II
c) III
d) IV
e) V
f) VI
g) VII

Terminology Index

Accelerando - Becoming gradually faster
Adagio - Slow, leisurely
Allegro - Lively
Andante - At a walking pace

Capo - The beginning
Crescendo - Becoming gradually louder

Da Capo - From the beginning
Decrescendo - Becoming gradually softer

Fine - The end
Forte - Loud
Fortissimo - Very loud

Legato - Smooth
Legatissimo - As smoothly as possible

Marcia - A march
Mezzo forte (mf) - Moderately loud
Mezzo piano (mp) - Moderately soft

Ostinato - Frequently repeated
Ottava - Octave

Piano (p) - Soft
Pianissimo (pp) - very softly

Staccato - Detached

Tempo - The speed
Tempo primo - Hold the original speed
Tenuto - Held
Tremolo (trem.) - The rapid repetition of a note, or rapid alternation of two notes.

Vibrato - Vibrating
Voce - Voice

Bibliography

Rudiments and Theory of music: The associated board of the royal schools of music (1958), 14 Bedford Square, London, WC1B 3JG

The right way to read music: Harry and Michael Baxter (2008) Constable + Robinson LTD, 169 Fulham Palace Road, London, W6 9ER

Learning to read Music—How to make sense of those mysterious symbols and bring music alive: Peter Nickol (2009) 3rd edition—How to books LTD, Oxford OX5 1RX

It's easy to bluff . . . Music theory - Joe Bennett (2000) Wise publications

www.enjoythemusic.com/
musicdefinition.html—accessed 1st
march 2011

www.dolmetsch.com/defst3.
html—accessed 1st march 2011